MW00379822

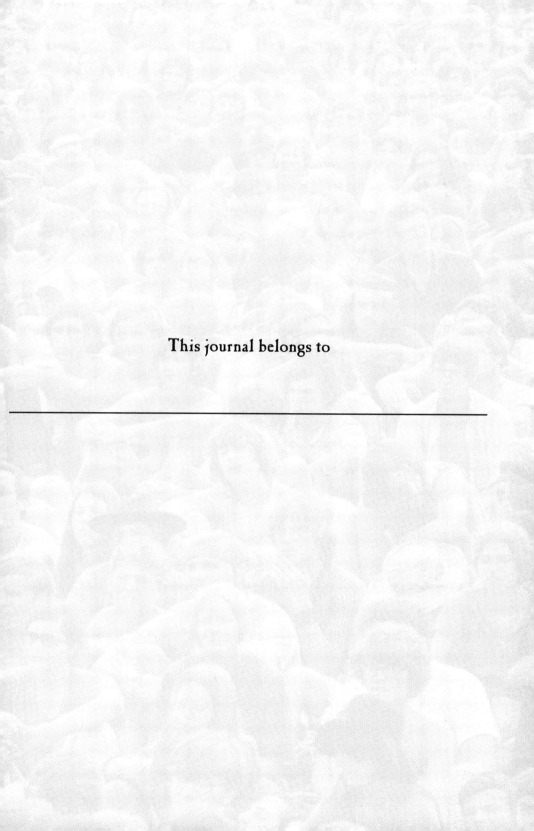

This journal belongs to

"I SAY, FOLLOW YOUR BLISS AND DON'T BE AFRAID,
AND DOORS WILL OPEN WHERE YOU DIDN'T KNOW
THEY WERE GOING TO BE."

—JOSEPH CAMPBELL

LOVERS
DREAMERS
& ARTISTS.

MAKE LOVE NOT WAR

"[IN THE 1960s] WE WERE YOUNG, WE WERE RECKLESS, ARROGANT, SILLY, HEADSTRONG ... AND WE WERE RIGHT! I REGRET NOTHING!"

—ABBIE HOFFMAN

LOVERS
DREAMERS
&ARTISTS.

MAKE LOVE NOT WAR

"THINK FOR YOURSELF AND QUESTION AUTHORITY."

—TIMOTHY LEARY

LOVERS
DREAMERS
&ARTISTS.

MAKE LOVE NOT WAR

"PEACE CAN BE MADE ONLY BY THOSE WHO ARE PEACEFUL,
AND LOVE CAN BE SHOWN ONLY BY THOSE WHO LOVE."

—ALAN WATTS

LOVERS
DREAMERS
&ARTISTS...

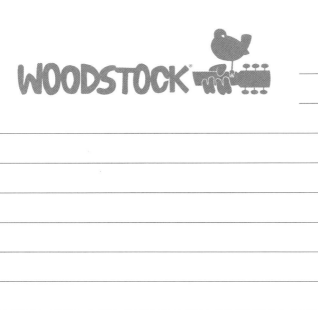

MAKE LOVE NOT WAR

"LIKE WOW, THESE PEOPLE ARE REALLY BEAUTIFUL,
THE COPS, THE STOREKEEPERS, THE ARMY, EVERYBODY."
—LAURA GLAZER, A WOODSTOCK ATTENDEE

LOVERS
DREAMERS
&ARTISTS.

MAKE LOVE NOT WAR

"DON'T BOTHER MAX'S COWS. LET THEM MOO IN PEACE."

—SIGN AT **W**OODSTOCK

LOVERS
DREAMERS
&ARTISTS

MAKE LOVE NOT WAR

"GOOD MORNING! WHAT WE HAVE IN MIND IS
BREAKFAST IN BED FOR 400,000."

—**WAVY GRAVY,** SPEAKING FROM THE STAGE

LOVERS
DREAMERS
&ARTISTS.

MAKE LOVE NOT WAR

"THE WHOLE THING IS A GAS. I DIG IT ALL, THE MUD, THE RAIN, THE MUSIC, THE HASSLES."

—Speed, a Woodstock attendee

LOVERS
DREAMERS
&ARTISTS.

MAKE LOVE NOT WAR

"I'M NOT WORRIED ABOUT THE SECURITY PARTICULARLY. IF PEOPLE HAVE ENOUGH TO DO, THERE WON'T BE TROUBLE."

—WESLEY A. POMEROY, HEAD OF SECURITY AT WOODSTOCK

LOVERS
DREAMERS
& ARTISTS.

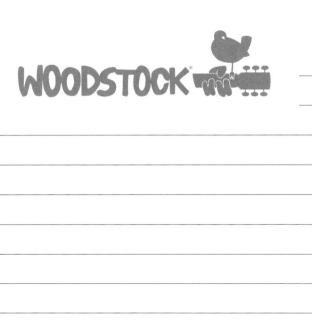